CW00487199

1. Soldiers of the 82nd Airborne Division cross-train Egyptian paratroops with .45 pistols, during the 1982 'Bright Star' manoeuvres. The Americans wear Daytime Desert BDUs with hats and Vietnam-era jungle boots. The latter are now limited-standard, but are still preferred for hot climate wear. (US Army via *Defense Image*)

UNIFORMS ILLUSTRATED No 16

MODERN AMERICAN SOLDIER

ARNOLD MEISNER & LEE RUSSELL

ARMS AND ARMOUR PRESS

Introduction

Published in 1986 by Arms & Armour Press Ltd.,
2–6 Hampstead High Street, London NW3 1QQ.

Distributed in the United States by Sterling
Publishing Co. Inc., 2 Park Avenue, New York,
N.Y. 10016.

British Library Cataloguing in Publication Data:
Meisner, Arnold
Modern American soldier. – (Uniforms
illustrated; 16)
1. United States. *Army* – Uniforms
I. Title   II. Russell, Lee E.   III. Series
355.1′4′0973   UC483

ISBN 0-85368-762-5

Editing, design and artwork by Roger Chesneau.
Typesetting by Typesetters (Birmingham) Ltd.
Printed and bound in Italy by GEA/GEP in
association with Keats European Ltd., London.

◀2
2. The United States Military Academy at West Point
issues a wide variety of uniforms to its Cadet Corps,
from the most traditional dress and ceremonial
uniforms to preppie-style collegiate clothes and
ordinary BDUs. These members of a cadet colour
party wear the very formal Full Dress Grey Over
White Uniform Under Arms, comprising the pale
grey ('Cadet Grey') full dress coat worn with black
'tarbucket' shako and white trousers. Although this
photograph was taken in 1958, the uniform remains
unchanged. It is the most traditional American
military uniform and dates back to the War of 1812.
(US Army)

The purpose of this book is to take a brief look at US Army
uniforms applicable to the 1980s. It does not purport to be a
study in depth, but it will provide basic information for the
researcher, costume designer and miniature figure painter. For
this reason, some esoteric formal dress (such as mess uniforms
for enlisted personnel) has been omitted in favour of field
clothing and equipment. It should be remembered that the
average soldier, even officer, wears only the basic Class 'A' and
'B' Uniforms and BDUs for most of the year, and may only be
vaguely aware of some of the more formal wear. However, a
few discontinued items, such as the Army Tan Uniform, are
covered in this volume for the benefit of readers who may not
be aware of their status.

The many medals, badges, patches and tabs, profusely
issued by the Army and a source of some confusion, even to the
wearers, are discussed only casually, owing to lack of space.
The US Army has often been accused of 'trying to find some
doodad to put on every blank spot on the uniform' (a quotation
from a senior Army sergeant writing to the *Army Times*, by the
way), but the Army's Awards Program considers these
important to morale and so continues the policy.

The number of photographs devoted to female soldiers will
come as a surprise to some readers, but women now comprise
about ten per cent of the military personnel of the United
States, and, in the Army, serve in 321 of the 376 enlisted
occupation specialities and in 202 of the 211 officer career
fields. They are expected to carry out their duties, even well
into pregnancy.

The authors wish to thank the following, for their assistance
in the preparation of this book: LTC Paul Knox and Major
Mike Hagstrom of the Army Public Affairs Office, New York
City; Mr Jeff Lindblad and Mr William U. Rosenmund, of the
Office, Chief of Public Affairs, Washington, DC; the Staff of
Soldiers Magazine; Mr Severino Mendez; Mr Steve Zaloga; Mr
George Balin; 1LT Wim Roemersma (New York National
Guard); Major Charles Spyker, FORSCOM PAO; Colonel
John McNeil and CPT George Wright, 24th Infantry Division
PAO; Major Robert Percival, 9th Infantry Division PAO;
Major Robert Chesley, 25th Infantry Division PAO; Mr John
Fairbank, WESTCOM PAO; Major Jim Burns, EUCOM
PAO; Ms Andrea Hamburger, USMA PAO; Mr Rick Boeth,
Time Magazine; Mr Guy Cooper of *Newsweek Magazine*; and a
lot of ordinary soldiers, in various parts of the country, who
answered some very strange questions so quickly over the
telephone. Finally, thanks are also due to Mr Andreas
Constantinou and Mr Sam Katz for their technical and
administrative assistance, which literally made this book
possible. It should be stressed that all the opinions in the book,
as well as any errors or omissions, are the responsibility of the
authors.

Arnold Meisner wishes to dedicate this book to his mother
and father, and Lee Russell wishes to include a dedication to
Mr Roland Garcia, who started this all so long ago with a box
of toy soldiers.

Arnold Meisner and Lee Russell

3. The current service uniform for male personnel is the AG-344 (Army Green, Shade 344). It is authorized for year-round wear, and, when worn with the jacket, it is referred to as the Class 'A' Uniform. Shown here is the version for officers, colonels and below (including warrant officers). It differs from the enlisted man's uniform in having black mohair bands added to the cuffs and along the outer seams of the trousers. These officers, attending an awards ceremony at Fort Benning, Georgia, in October 1966, also show a selection of the insignia and badges authorized with the Class 'A' Uniform. (US Army)

4. General William C. Westmoreland, serving as Army Chief of Staff, with Sergeant-Major of the Army George W. Dunaway, at a Pentagon ceremony in August 1968. General Westmoreland wears the AG-344 Uniform for General Officers, which has wider cuff braid than that for other officers and a double stripe down the trouser leg rather than a single stripe. In the American Army, generals have no specific branch (in one of the literal meanings of 'general officer'), so no branch insignia are worn on the lower lapel. (US Army)

5. Colonel Moohad Mooradian, Commander of the Division Support Command, 25th Infantry Division, at Schofield Barracks, Hawaii, in May, 1982. His officers' 'US' and Quartermaster Branch insignia are worn on his lapels, and insignia of rank, a silver eagle, on his epaulettes. Also worn on the epaulettes are the distinctive insignia or 'unit crests' of his organization, the 25th Division's DISCOM in this case. They are pinned through green felt combat leader's identification loops, indicating that the wearer directly commands combat troops. (US Army via *Defense Image*)

▲3　▼4　　　　5▶

▲6   ▼7

CHARLESTON

6. Major-General Charles W. Dyke, Commanding General of the 8th Infantry Division (Mech.) at Bad Kreuznach, Germany, 1984, wearing the large number of badges and individual decorations typical of senior officers and enlisted personnel. They indicate that the general is both Airborne- and Ranger-qualified, and has served on both the Army and Joint General Staffs. Perhaps his most impressive award, however, is the blue and silver Combat Infantry Badge worn above all his other decorations on his left breast. (US Army via *Defense Image*)

7. A first lieutenant of the 3rd Infantry Regiment, 'The Old Guard', serving in Washington, DC, in 1982. With his Army Green Uniform, he wears the officers' service hat, the version prescribed for company-grade officers (i.e. captains and below). The same hat is also worn by warrant officers, but the service hat for majors and above has a visor decorated with gold oak leaves. The hat device, the Coat of Arms of the United States, is the same for all commissioned officers, second lieutenants up to generals, but warrant officers have an eagle of a different pattern. On his lapels, the lieutenant displays his officers' 'US' and Infantry Branch devices; the upper quadrant of the latter also displays the regimental number, a permitted variation but one seldom seen. The unit crests of the 3rd Infantry Regiment are secured through combat leader's identification loops, and an Infantry cord is worn on the right shoulder. (US Army)

8. A staff sergeant assigned to Wynn Army Hospital, Fort Steward, Georgia, in May 1985, wears the enlisted version of the AG-344 Class 'A' Uniform. Although an enlisted version of the service hat is available as an optional purchase item, the garrison cap is more commonly worn, as here. (The officers' garrison cap is similar, but trimmed in silver and black for warrant officers, in gold and black for commissioned officers and in gold for generals.) On the sergeant's lapels are worn an enlisted 'US' device on the right lapel and enlisted branch insignia (here, a Medical Corps caduceus) on the left. His shoulder patch and unit crests are those of the Army's Health Services Command, worn by all personnel assigned to Army hospitals, and his service stripes denote nine years of service. The badge is an Expert Marksman's Badge with Rifle and Pistol Bars. All US Army medical personnel now qualify with weapons, and carry them in the field. (Arnold Meisner/*Defense Image*)

9. A Specialist 4, also assigned to Wynn Army Hospital, May 1985. His rank is the last remains of a system originally set up in the 1950s to distinguish enlisted personnel holding 'technical' positions from those in 'command' slots. At one time, there were Specialist equivalents to every enlisted grade above Private First Class, but gradually all were converted to NCO status except for this one rank, equivalent to Corporal. The SP/4's Marksman's Badges show weapons proficiency at the Sharpshooter and Marksman level, left to right respectively. (Arnold Meisner/*Defense Image*)

10. The AG-344 Army Green Class 'A' 'Classic' Uniform for Women Officers, modelled by an Army nurse assigned to Wynn, May 1985. Black mohair braid is worn at the cuffs only, not on the skirt or slacks. A female general, of whom there are several, would wear the wider braid authorized for general officers. Women officers also wear their 'US' and branch insignia in a different manner from their male counterparts, the 'US' device being worn on the right lapel and the branch insignia (here, that of the Army Nurse Corps) on the left. The women officers' service hat (commonly called the 'pop hat') is the same for warrant and commissioned officers below the rank of Major, women field-grade and general officers wearing a gold oak leaf decoration instead of the gold embroidered hat band. All women personnel wear an AG-415 shirt and black necktab with this uniform. (Arnold Meisner/*Defense Image*)

11. A woman staff sergeant wearing the enlisted version of the AG-344 'Classic' Class 'A' Uniform, together with the enlisted women's garrison cap; again, there is an optional private-purchase version of the service hat for enlisted women, but it is rarely seen. The Health Services Command shoulder patch and unit crests are worn in the same fashion as on the men's uniform. (Arnold Meisner/*Defense Image*)

8▲   9▼

10▲   11▼

▲12

▲13 ▼14

12. The AG-344 'Classic' Uniform, worn with slacks. In the early 1980s this supplanted two older uniforms, one a skirt and jacket and the other a pantsuit, both in AG-344 material. The positions of the enlisted 'US' and branch insignia follow those of the male uniform, as does the position of service stripes and chevrons (although the last two are made in a smaller size for women). Note the sergeant's Expert Marksman's Badge; all female personnel currently qualify with basic weapons. (Arnold Meisner/*Defense Image*)

13. The Army Class 'B' Uniform for Male Officers consists of the AG-415 light green shirt with black tie, AG-344 trousers and service hat. The shirt comes in both long- and short-sleeve versions and, again, the officers' garrison cap may be worn. Officers and NCOs, sergeants and above, wear their rank insignia as cloth slip-on devices on the epaulettes. At the time this photograph was taken (1982), unit crests were worn on both epaulettes and above the right pocket, but they are now no longer worn with any Class 'B' uniform. (US Army)

14. The Class 'B' Uniform for Enlisted Men, as worn with the short-sleeve AG-415 shirt and enlisted garrison cap. Personnel below the grade of Sergeant wear their rank insignia as metal pin-on devices on the shirt collar, sergeants and above wearing the cloth slip-on type on their epaulettes. Distinctive insignia (here, the Health Services Command crest) are worn on the left side of the garrison cap. Aside from the name-tag, no badges or medals of any kind are authorized to be worn with the Class 'B' Uniform. (Arnold Meisner/*Defense Image*)

◀15   16▲

15. The current Class 'B' Uniform replaced two older tan-khaki uniforms, in cotton for enlisted men and in a polyester–cotton mixture called 'TW' (or Tropical Weave) for officers, shown here. All badges and decorations could be worn with this uniform: officers wore metal pin-on rank and branch insignia on their collars and unit crests on their epaulettes; enlisted men wore 'US' and branch insignia in the same place and full-colour chevrons on the sleeves. Authorized headgear was either the service hat or the garrison cap. Although the dress belt buckle was specified for this uniform, for some reason this Infantry captain wears the black frame subdued buckle usually worn with field uniforms. Both versions of the Army Tan Uniform were phased out in September 1985. (US Army)

16. The Class 'B' Uniform for Women Officers consists of the AG-415 shirt and the skirt or slacks of the AG-344 'Classic' Uniform, worn with the service hat. Rank is displayed by means of slip-on devices on the epaulettes. (Arnold Meisner/*Defense Image*)

◀17 ▲18 ▼19

17. As mentioned in the Introduction, women soldiers are expected to perform their duties well into pregnancy, and the Army provides maternity uniforms when necessary. This is the Class 'B' version, as modelled by an SP/4; the Class 'A' version is a sleeveless smock in AG-344 material. The Army also provides a Maternity Work Uniform in camouflage material, and even a special version of its chemical, biological and radiological protective clothing for pregnant personnel. (Arnold Meisner/*Defense Image*)

18. The Class 'B' Uniform for Enlisted Women. As with the men, NCOs display rank insignia as slip-on devices on the epaulettes, and personnel below the grade of Sergeant wear metal pin-on devices on the collar. Only privates have no insignia. (Arnold Meisner/*Defense Image*)

19. The Class 'B' versions of the Women's 'Classic' Uniform supplanted no fewer than three older uniforms, two of which are shown in this 1979 photograph – the AG-388 Skirt and Jacket Uniform, as worn by the corporal in front, and the 1950s Green Cord (Shade 160) Uniform, as worn by the private behind her. There was also a dress-style uniform in the bright green AG-388 colour. As with the equivalent men's Army Tan Uniform, all decorations and badges could be worn with these uniforms. The women wear the black beret authorized for female personnel since the mid-1970s. All AG-388 uniforms were scheduled to be phased out in September 1986. (Lee E. Russell)

20. The Army black raincoat is the authorized outer garment for wear in inclement weather. It has a zip-in liner of polyester–nylon material for additional warmth if required. This soldier wears the optional enlisted men's service hat (usually called the 'saucer hat') with his AG-344 Class 'A' Uniform. At the time of this photograph, 1974, no decision had yet been made on the wearing of insignia with the raincoat. (US Army)

20 ▶

21. Eventually, the Army decided that enlisted rank insignia would be worn as metal pin-on devices on the raincoat collar, while officers would wear metal pin-on insignia on the epaulettes. (Arnold Meisner/*Defense Image*)

22. The women's version of the Army black raincoat, and the women's black beret, as worn by a sergeant. (US Army)

23. A black zippered jacket is also worn as an outer garment in cool weather, by both male and female personnel (in this instance an Army nurse officer). Rank insignia are worn as metal pin-on devices on both lapels, and on the left side of the women officers' garrison cap, with its silver and black piping. (Arnold Meisner/*Defense Image*)

24. Enlisted personnel wear rank insignia as pin-on devices on the collar of the zippered jacket, as shown by this Specialist 4 of the Wynn Army Hospital, May 1985. (Arnold Meisner/*Defense Image*)

◀ 21

◀22   23▲   24▼

▲25

▲26 27▶   28▶▶

25. Another item of clothing authorized for wear in inclement weather is the Army black sweater, a V-necked garment with reinforcing patches at shoulders and elbows. The presentation of rank as slip-on devices for NCOs is well shown in this photograph. (US Army)

26. Women personnel also wear the Army black sweater. At the time of this photograph (May 1985) the unit crest was authorized for wear on this garment, but permission for this has now been withdrawn. (Arnold Meisner/*Defense Image*)

27. The Army Blue Uniform for Male Officers, here modelled by an Infantry captain. This is a formal uniform, made in Army Blue Shade 150 material, with all trim in gold. Its possession is mandatory for all serving officers. The colour of the trousers is a light blue shade for everyone below the rank of Brigadier-General, and the single 1½in gold stripe is the same for all male personnel, colonels and below. Officers' insignia of rank are displayed on

nineteenth century-style shoulder straps. Branch is displayed in three ways: conventional pin-on metal devices are worn on the lower lapels, while the branch colour appears both as a background for the shoulder straps and as gold-bordered bands on the hat and sleeves. (US Army)

28. The Army Blue Uniform for a field-grade officer (here, a Major of Artillery) differs little from that of a company-grade officer, the oak-leaf trim to the visor of the hat being the only essential change. This trim is worn by all officers above the rank of Major. The Army Blue Uniform for general officers differs slightly from that for field-grade officers. Trousers are dark blue to match the coat, and two ¾in gold trouser stripes are worn rather than the usual single stripe. Moreover, American generals technically have no specific branch, and only the 'US' insignia are worn on the lapels. Generals' uniforms are also trimmed in blue-black velvet instead of a branch colour on shoulder straps, sleeves and hat. (US Army)

29. A close-up photograph showing the position of insignia and decorations on the Officer's Army Blue Unifrom, this time for an Infantry officer serving with 'The Old Guard', the 3rd Infantry Regiment, in Washington DC in 1982. Infantry branch is shown in several ways, one being the light blue Infantry cord at the right shoulder. The cost of the Army Blue Uniform is one of the financial headaches faced by newly commissioned officers. The uniform is expensive, he is required to have it, yet only in units like 'The Old Guard' would he have a chance to wear it more than once or twice a year. (US Army)

30. The Army Blue Uniform for Enlisted Men also consists of a dark blue (Army Shade 150) jacket and light blue trousers decorated with a gold stripe. Chevrons of standard size are worn on the sleeves, but service stripes are oversize on this uniform and worn on both sleeves. As with officers, a white shirt and black tie are worn. (US Army)

31. The Army Blue Uniform can also be worn with a black bow tie, in which case it corresponds to a civilian tuxedo. Enlisted personnel are generally not required to have the Army Blue Uniform, and even those who elect to purchase it usually avoid buying the hat, since the average soldier would only wear the uniform indoors at some formal event. (Arnold Meisner/*Defense Image*)

32. The wearing of insignia, badges and decorations with the Enlisted Army Blue Uniform is shown in this photograph of a 3rd Infantry enlisted man, circa 1982. All trim is in gold, and the branch colour does not appear at all. Enlisted 'US' and branch insignia are worn on the lapels in the same fashion as on the Army green jacket. Infantry personnel only are authorized to wear both of these devices, as well as the hat device, on a light blue plastic backing as shown, along with the Infantry cord. (US Army)

33. Soldiers of the 3rd Infantry Regiment march in the Armed Forces Day Parade in New York City, May 1978. Members of the 3rd are among the few enlisted men to be actually issued with the Army Blue Uniform, which is required for their ceremonial duties. The fixed bayonets of their M14 rifles are also a tradition: the 3rd is the only regiment authorized to pass in review with fixed bayonets, in honour of their courage at the Battle of Cerro Gordo in the Mexican War. (Lee E. Russell)

31▲

32▲ 33▼

34. The Army Blue Uniform for Women Officers consists of a dark blue (Army Shade 150) skirt and jacket, worn with a white shirt and black necktab. Branch colours, here the maroon of the Army's Medical Branch, are displayed only on the sleeve, whilst the hat is simply a blue version of the women officers' service hat. Branch insignia are worn as on the Class 'A' Uniform, with the 'US' device on the right lapel and the branch device on the left. (Arnold Meisner/*Defense Image*)

35. Another view of the Women Officers' Army Blue Uniform, here worn by a major. Her branch, the Adjutant General Corps, is shown by the shield-shaped device on her lapel, and by the dark blue bands on her jacket sleeves. Women officers may hold commissions in any branch except the combat arms of Infantry, Armor and Artillery. (US Army)

36. The Army White Uniform, here worn by a 3rd Infantry major, is an optional uniform for warm-weather wear by both officers and enlisted personnel. A black bow tie can be worn with it to make it the equivalent of a civilian summer tuxedo. Except for the colour, the uniform is identical to the standard AG-344 Class 'A' Uniform for both officers and enlisted men, although the officers' trousers are plain, without stripes. The only difference in the wear of insignia applies to the Enlisted Uniform, where the oversize service stripes, as on the Army Blue Uniform, are worn on both sleeves. Female officer and enlisted equivalents are similarly white versions of the Women's AG-344 Skirt and Jacket Uniform. (US Army)

37. The standard US Army uniform for wear in combat and field environments is the BDU or Battle Dress Uniform. Also worn as everyday dress in garrison, it was even chosen by Major-General William H. Schneider, Commanding General of the 24th Infantry Division, Schofield Barracks, Hawaii, for his official photograph in August 1982. Made of a 50/50 nylon-cotton mix (the nylon component is for protection against flash burns), the fabric is printed in a four-colour disruptive camouflage called 'the woodland pattern'. All insignia worn with this uniform are of the 'subdued' type, black on olive drab material. A 'US Army' name-tape is worn over the left pocket and the soldier's last name over the right. Any combat or special skill badges, such as the General's Parachute Badge, may also be worn in subdued material. Shoulder patches, both those of the wearer's current organization and of any with which he might have served during wartime, are also worn in subdued material on the sleeves. All personnel, from privates to generals, wear insignia of rank on the jacket's lapel, although the presentation varies slightly for different ranks. General Schneider wears his two-star rank insignia on both lapels; officers, colonels and below, would wear subdued branch insignia on the left lapel and their rank on the right. Black metal pin-on rank insignia, which can be removed in combat, can also be worn instead. Suspended from the General's buttonhole is a plastic case for earplugs, often worn by personnel whose duties involve being close to artillery. (US Army via *Defense Image*)

◄37

38. The BDU, here worn by personnel of the 24th Infantry Division during a change-of-command ceremony at Fort Stewart, Georgia, in May 1985. After its introduction, several problems with the BDUs manifested themselves, mostly relating to its appearance. To prevent undue wear on the nylon-cotton cloth, soldiers were ordered not to starch or iron the uniform, and this, coupled with its originally generous cut, often resulted in a somewhat slovenly appearance, out of keeping with the previous standards of garrison dress. Consequently, many soldiers took it on themsleves to have their uniforms altered, with a view toward improving their appearance (several of the uniforms in this photograph show evidence of unauthorized tailoring). Eventually, the Army decided to permit ironing, and to make some alterations to the basic uniform to make it more presentable in the garrison environment. (Arnold Meisner/*Defense Image*)

39. Male and female officers of the 24th Infantry Divison at Fort Stewart, May 1985. Current Army policy makes few concessions to women soldiers in the field, and they are issued with exactly the same uniforms as the men. (Arnold Meisner/*Defense Image*)

38▲   39▼

▲ 40

▲ 41 ▼ 42

40. The BDU includes a 'woodland' camouflage cap, actually a BDU version of the old M1951 'patrol cap' originally made in plain olive drab. Here it is worn by a private of the 11th Armored Cavalry Regiment, in Fulda, Germany; he is adjusting a TOW missile sight. All ranks, from Private to General, wear rank insignia on caps, either cloth or subdued metal pin-on types. (US Army)

41. US Army Special Forces soldiers ('Green Berets') of the 12th Special Forces Group (Airborne) after a jump in Korea, March 1984. OD field sweaters and wool shirts are worn beneath their BDUs, and the man at the right wears an M65 field jacket as well. The Special Forces are one of three élite units authorized to wear berets, which in this case are coloured rifle green. On the beret is the shield-shaped group 'flash'; officers wear rank insignia on the flash, whereas NCOs and enlisted men wear the Special Forces unit crest. The beret is not a normal field item (the BDU cap is normally worn), so full-colour items are permitted. The sergeant on the right wears a 'Special Forces' tab above his shoulder patch, indicating complete SF qualification, while his companions either have not yet qualified or, more likely, have simply not bothered to sew on the tab. The men wear a mixture of M1956 and LC-1 web gear, and the sergeant has attached a pilot's survival knife to one strap of his equipment. (Arnold Meisner/*Defense Image*)

42. A private first class of the 1st Cavalry Division (currently an armoured division based at Fort Hood, Texas) prepares to use his Redeye anti-aircraft launcher during a III Corps competition, June 1982. Note the reinforcement patches at the elbows of his BDU jacket, a feature designed to reduce wear on the uniform. A black metal PFC device is attached to his M1 helmet's camouflage cover. (US Army)

43. Personnel assigned to Wynn Army Hospital, Fort Stewart, Georgia, model the Enlisted Men's Army Blue Uniform (left) and the Women Officers' Army Blue Uniform (right). (Arnold Meisner/*Defense Image*)

43 ▶

▲44 ▼45

44. Wynn Army Hospital personnel in Army Green Class 'A' Uniform: (left to right) the Enlisted Women's 'Classic' Uniform, with garrison cap; the Enlisted Men's AG-344 Uniform, with garrison cap; and the Women Officers' 'Classic' Uniform, with service ('pot') hat. Shirts are AG-415 Green and all accessories are black. (Arnold Meisner/*Defen Image*)

45. The Class 'B' Uniform for (left to right) Enlisted Women Enlisted Men, and Women Officers. (Arnold Meisner/*Defen Image*)

46. A colour party of Army drill instructors, assigned to basic traini units at Fort Bliss, Texas, during a change of command ceremony March 1985. Their dril sergeant's hats (usually called 'Smokey the Bea hats') are worn with BDUs and light blue Infantry branch scarves and black combat boots with white lacing. The brass buckles worn wit their pistol belts displa the Drill Instructor's Badge. (Arnold Meisner/*Defense Image*

47. Army Reservists of Ohio's 83rd ARCOM (Army Reserve Command) relax with coffee and cigarettes during the 'Reforger 8 manoeuvres in Germany. They wear BDUs with a mix of M and BDU field jackets, ALICE gear and M17 protective masks. (Arnold Meisner/*Defen Image*)

48. Heavily burdened infantrymen of the 25t Infantry Division ('Tropic Lightning') take up positions durin Operation 'Team Spiri Korea, 1984. The ALICE medium pack, entrenching tool carrie and M17 protective mask carrier are shown from several angles. T soldier in the immedia foreground carries a ro of communications wi attached to his pack. (Arnold Meisner/*Defen Image*)

46 ▲

47 ▲   48 ▼

◀49

50▲ 51▼

52▲

49. Special Forces personnel of the 7th Special Forces Group, Fort Bragg, North Carolina, with climbing equipment. The Special Forces are the last major users of the leaf-pattern Jungle Fatigue Uniform, originally issued first to élite troops in Vietnam. The jungle boots are also being phased out, as stocks on the inventory decline. The green beret and full-colour 'flash' are not normal field wear, and usually an M1951 field hat or BDU cap is worn. (US Army)

50. A second lieutenant of the 25th Infantry Division ('Tropic Lightning'), during Operation 'Team Spirit' in Korea, March 1984. He wears the BDU in the field over an OG-106 wool shirt and trousers. A subdued metal rank device is pinned to the front of his M1 helmet's 'woodland' camouflage cover. The device attached to the muzzle of his M16 is a blank firing adaptor used for the manoeuvres. The black leather gloves and OD wool inserts are also worn with the Dress Uniform in winter. (Arnold Meisner/*Defense Image*)

51. General Robert W. Sennewald, Commander of the 8th US Army in Korea at the time this photograph was taken, wearing the new BDU camouflage field jacket and BDU cap. The new field jacket is virtually identical in cut to the older M65 type worn by the officer visible behind the general, but it is made in a 50/50 nylon-cotton mix and, like all other components of the BDU, incorporates special dyes in the fabric to reduce its infra-red signature. All officers wear rank insignia on the epaulettes of the field jacket, enlisted personnel having them on the collar. General Sennewald is also wearing the special leather dress belt and buckle issued to general officers. (Arnold Meisner/*Defense Image*)

52. Troops of the 25th Infantry Division disembark from a chartered commercial airliner for the 'Team Spirit' manoeuvres in Korea, March 1984. Note that one of the officers in the foreground, the captain on the right, wears green combat leader's identification loops on the epaulettes of his field jacket. (Arnold Meisner/*Defense Image*)

29

53. One recently procured item is the new Army combat boot, adopted after several years of testing to replace the current boot. Made of black leather, it incorporates 'speedlace' pegs rather than eyelets, and its direct moulded sole is made with wide 'Panama' treads to reduce the build-up of mud and dirt. (US Army)

54. The Army intended to use the BDU for wear all year round, but several features, notably the hot nylon-cotton fabric, made the uniform unsuitable for warm weather, a problem brought most forcibly to light during Operation 'Urgent Fury', the attack on Grenada. Eventually the Army's Natick Laboratories designed a warm-weather BDU, made entirely of cotton, which also eliminated some of the original BDU's less desirable features, including its baggy fit. As an interim measure, however, the Army decided to issue the large stocks of Vietnam-era jungle fatigues it had been holding in storage, starting in 1983. These 101st Airborne (Air Assault) artillerymen are wearing this uniform, together with M17 protective masks in carriers and (centre soldier) an Army rain jacket. (Arnold Meisner/*Defense Image*)

55. An XVIII Airborne Corps captain, wearing Vietnam-vintage jungle fatigues at Fort Stewart, Georgia, May 1985. The slanted pockets create some problems in positioning insignia. This officer wears his name-tapes according to regulations, parallel to the ground rather than following the top of the pockets; one special skill badge, his Parachutist Wings, is worn above his left name-tape while a second, a Scuba Badge, is worn on the pocket flap itself. With the adoption of the BDU the Army introduced a new method of rolling up the sleeves, to keep the camouflaged portion outermost, and the officer here has carried this out with the jungle fatigues, although it is rather pointless with an all-OD uniform. Since the late 1970s, with one brief gap, US paratroops have been authorized to wear a red beret and, although officially a dress item, it is often seen in the field. A flash in the full regimental colours is worn on the beret, with either a rank device (for officers) or a unit crest (for enlisted men) pinned to the centre. (Arnold Meisner/*Defense Image*)

▲53   ▼54   55▶

▲56 ▼57

56. The US Army Rangers are the third category of troops to be authorized berets, in this case black ones. Rangers are élite light infantry, descended from the Second World War American equivalent of the British Commandos. As with the Special Forces and Airborne troops, they wear full-colour flashes with either rank insignia or unit crests on their berets. It should be noted that this photograph is of a ceremony in garrison; unlike the Airborne and Special Forces troopers, Rangers *never* take their berets into the field. (US Army)

57. The Army Rangers have their own distinctive headgear for combat wear. These men, members of the 1st Battalion, 75th Infantry Regiment (Ranger), proudly wear the old M1951 field cap (sometimes called a 'patrol cap'). While the rest of the Army wears the BDU camouflage cap, the Rangers are the last unit to retain the plain OD model, now folded in a distinctive fashion. The photograph also shows a good rear view of the nylon LC-1 belt suspenders, with their 'Y'-pattern layout. (Arnold Meisner/*Defense Image*)

58▲

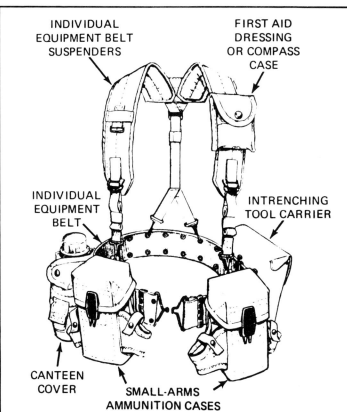

INDIVIDUAL
EQUIPMENT BELT
SUSPENDERS

FIRST AID
DRESSING
OR COMPASS
CASE

INDIVIDUAL
EQUIPMENT
BELT

INTRENCHING
TOOL CARRIER

CANTEEN
COVER

SMALL-ARMS
AMMUNITION CASES

◀59

58. Two Army Rangers of the 2nd Battalion, 75th Infantry, examine an assortment of captured Communist small-arms in Grenada, October 1983. The distinctive 'Ranger crush' of the M1951 field cap is shown from another angle. At the time, a commercial manufacturer had arranged with the US Government for the gratis issue of his load-bearing vests to members of 2/75, and many of these were used in Grenada, as shown by the man on the right. Note also the subdued 'Ranger' tab and Parachute Badge worn on the field cap. (US Army)
59. The assembled components of the current Army web gear, designated ALICE (All-Purpose Lightweight Individual Combat Equipment), are shown here in a page from an Army equipment manual; at present, a second canteen is also worn. Some variation may be seen in the positioning of individual components, but most units specify which item is to be worn, and where. (US Army)

60. A captain of the 101st Airborne Division (Air Assault), wearing the standard set of ALICE equipment in the field. His OD jungle fatigues are worn with subdued name-tapes, insignia and shoulder patch, as previously described, and include a Jungle Expert patch on the left pocket, indicating that he is a graduate of the Army's Jungle Warfare School in Panama. (Arnold Meisner/*Defense Image*)

61. Another view of the ALICE equipment, here worn with BDUs, is shown in this photograph of a private first class of Company 'C', 509th Infantry (Pathfinder, Airborne), assigned to Fort Rucker, Alabama. The snap ring attached to the soldier's harness is used for 'rapelling' from helicopters and is the mark of Airborne and Air Assault soldiers. A private-purchase knife is worn attached to the LC-1 pistol belt, just behind the left ammunition pouch, and the sew-on rank insignia on the BDU jacket is also noteworthy. Most Airborne personnel use this pattern insignia, since the metal devices can cut the wearer's face during parachute jumps. The weapon is an M72 LAW (Light Anti-Tank Weapon) launcher, soon to be replaced by the Swedish AT-4. (US Army)

62,63 Side, rear and detail views of the LC-1 medium combat field pack, usually called a rucksack, as worn with the ALICE equipment; an LC-1 or -2 packframe can be attached if necessary. The AN/PRC-77 radio can be carried in the special inside pocket, making the operator a less conspicuous target to snipers in combat. In addition to the main compartment and three external pockets, the outside of the pack includes nylon equipment hangers to attach a variety of other items. (US Army)

◀**60**

61▲   62▼   63▼

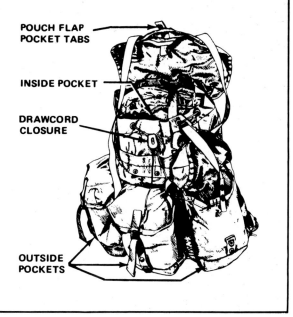

POUCH FLAP
POCKET TABS

INSIDE POCKET

DRAWCORD
CLOSURE

OUTSIDE
POCKETS

▲64 ▼65

66 ▲

◄67

64. 82nd Airborne Division troopers at the Point Salines Airport, Grenada, wearing ALICE medium packs with a variety of equipment attached: one- and two-quart canteens, entrenching tools and LAW anti-tank rockets are in view. Even to these superbly conditioned troopers, the weight of their packs is an obvious strain; several factors contribute to this, one being the high rate of fire of modern infantry weapons, and the consequent need to carry adequate ammunition. (US Army)

65. An M47 Dragon anti-tank gunner of the 25th Infantry Division ('Tropic Lightning') takes a break during training in Korea, March 1984. He has already removed one of the launcher's protective caps, and note also the extra LC-1 canteen attached to an equipment hanger on the right side of the pack. (Arnold Meisner/*Defense Image*)

66. A sergeant squad-leader of the 25th Infantry Division positions his men during Operation 'Team Spirit', Korea, 1984. Attached to his ALICE gear is what appears to be a personal radio, and also a scabbard for his M7 bayonet. In addition to the contents of his rucksack, items are stuffed into the cargo pockets of his BDU trousers. He also appears to be wearing chemical protective overboots over his normal footwear. (Arnold Meisner/*Defense Image*)

67. In the early 1980s the US Army began testing a new type of body armour to replace the M1952 and M1969 types then in service; at the same time, a new helmet was designed to replace the venerable M1, used by the Army since 1942. Both the helmet and the armour vest were made of kevlar, a revolutionary material which resists both shrapnel and bullet penetration, so that, although lighter in weight than the equipment they supplanted, the new items offered superior protection. The body armour is made with a 'woodland' pattern BDU finish, and includes shoulder pieces to secure the ALICE harness firmly in place. Together termed PASGT (Personal Armor System, Ground Troops), the helmet and armour were adopted by the Army, and general issue began in 1984. (US Army)

68. Among the first units to receive the new helmet – in fact it conducted the trials for it – was the 82nd Airborne Division at Fort Bragg, North Carolina. Paratroops are issued with a slightly different version of the 'Fritz', which differs in the details of its suspension. Other points of interest in this photograph are the taped flashlight and protective mask carrier, secured for jumping, and the snap ring. (Arnold Meisner/*Defense Image*)

69. A side view of the PASGT vest and helmet. The markedly Germanic appearance of the helmet quickly led to its being dubbed 'Fritz'. Early models were manufactured with an impregnated 'woodland' camouflage pattern, but later a cover was adopted instead and the helmets are now made in olive drab. (US Army)

70. Another 82nd soldier, this time a member of a military intelligence unit, carries out a simulated prisoner interrogation with a blindfolded 'suspect'; the 82nd patch on his right sleeve identifies him as a Grenada veteran. The American public got its first look at the new 'Fritz' helmet during 'Urgent Fury', and its appearance, together with the camouflaged BDUs, caused some surprise. One Second World War veteran even wrote to a national magazine to complain that he 'used to shoot at guys who looked like that', but, their appearance aside, the helmets saved the lives of two 82nd soldiers on Grenada. (Arnold Meisner/*Defense Image*)

71. The 'Fritz' helmet is now in service with most elements of the US Army, including these air defence Hawk missile crewmen in Germany, shown preparing their weapons while participating in Operation 'Certain Fury', part of the 'Reforger 84' excercises. Although an elastic band is usually issued to attach local foliage to the helmet, the soldier on the left seems to have improvised his own camouflage from something else. The men also wear M17 protective masks in the 'side-carry' position. (US Army)

◄**68**

69▲   70▲   71▼

72. An M47 Dragon gunner poses with his special jump pack, which holds both the missile and the gunner's personal M16. Below the T-10 reserve parachute is a canvas kit bag, which contains additional equipment. The prototype 'Fritz' PASGT helmet is worn, with its imprinted camouflage pattern. The white tee-shirt is no longer worn with combat clothing, having been replaced with one of light brown colour. (US Army)

73. On the 1980s battlefield American vehicle crews would wear components of a specially designed combat uniform. Here, a soldier models the basic garment, the combat vehicle crewmen's (CVC) coveralls. Made of flame-retardant Nomex fabric, they accept a removable liner which adds further insulation in cold weather. A special ballistic undergarment may be worn under the coveralls, to protect the wearer against fragments and spall should his vehicle's

armour be penetrated. In hot climates, or under NBC (nuclear-biological-chemical) warfare conditions, a special microclimate conditioning vest may also be worn: this circulates a cooling liquid which carries off excess body heat and allows crews to work at near-normal efficiency for long periods of time. The coveralls also incorporate a much-requested drop-seat, and there is a casualty extraction strap behind the shoulders to facilitate the removal of injured crewmen from vehicles. (US Army)

74. In cold weather the armour crewman wears a winter-weight Nomex jacket, also issued to aircrews. It includes an opening at the back to gain access to the casualty extraction strap. Here, the cold-weather, high-temperature resistant jacket (Aircrew and CVC) is worn with CVC coveralls and the current DH-132 kevlar CVC helmet. (US Army)

75. Further components of the CVC uniform include Nomex gloves, balaclava and face mask, shown here at a 1980 exhibition of combat clothing. The footwear is an experimental version of the traditional tankers' boots in which a spiral strap replaces the lacing; featuring also an 'inside-out' brown leather surface, it was not proceeded with. (US Army)

76. A close-up view of the DH-132 CVC helmet and goggles, worn by a 1st Cavalry Division tanker during Operation 'Aqua Marine', one of NATO's 'Autumn Forge' exercises, held during September 1983. In peacetime, to save wear on expensive Nomex uniforms, standard BDUs are donned in training. The M3A1 'grease gun' is still standard issue for tank crews, and some 57,000, originally manufactured during the Korean War, are held in reserve stocks. (US Army)

77. Men of the 3/5th Cavalry Scouts, 9th Infantry Division (Motorized), pose with their Kawasaki dirt bikes in front of an AH-1S attack helicopter, early 1985. They wear obsolete CVC helmets and normal BDUs, and carry M3 'grease guns'. Attached to the handlebars of their motorcycles are (left to right), an AN/PRC-77 radio, the little-seen ALICE small pack (usually called a 'buttpack') and a map case. Dirt bikes have been used by Army scout units since the early 1970s. (US Army via *Defense Image*)

◀**75**

76 ▲   77 ▼

78. During the early 1970s Army Aviation personnel wore this uniform of fire-resistant Nomex shirt and trousers, GS/FRP-2 gloves and SPH-4C flying helmet, shown here with the Army's lightweight flyers' jacket, also of Nomex. Full subdued name-tapes and patches were worn on the shirt, as with fatigue clothing, and all items were made in OG-106 colour (olive drab). In addition to the Army flying jacket, Air Force L-2B and MA-1 types could also be worn. These were made in sage green, reversible to international orange. Currently, Army pilots are issued with CWU-36 and CWU-45 (light- and heavyweight, respectively) jackets, and an Air Force aircrew name-tag is worn instead of sew-on insignia (see below). (US Army)

79. Army Rangers of the 1/75th Infantry prepare demolition materials, during training at their base, Fort Stewart, Georgia, in spring 1985. They wear OD jungle fatigues and M1951 field hats, the latter folded into the distinctive 'Ranger crush'. (Arnold Meisner/*Defense Image*)

80. M551 Sheridan crewmen of the 4th Battalion (ABN), 68th Armor (the 82nd Airborne Division's armour component), with .45 pistols and M3 'grease guns', during a Fort Bragg exhibition. Their red berets display their unit crest within the regimental 'flash'. (Arnold Meisner/*Defense Image*)

81. Aviators of the 24th Infantry Division answer Press questions at Fort Stewart, December 1984. Although the setting sun has made their flight suits turn a shade of brown, this photograph still offers a good view of insignia positions, for both the old and new (aircrew name-tag) system. Note also the revolver carried by the officer on the right, tucked into a holster sewn to his SRU-21 survival vest. (Arnold Meisner/*Defense Image*)

79▲

80▲ 81▼

▲82

▲83 ▼84

82. A soldier of the 25th Infantry Division wearing the winter parka with its fur-trimmed hood during 'Team Spirit', 1984. The orange band on his helmet is a manoeuvre marking. Face camouflage is an integral part of combat dress and is commonly applied during exercises of this nature. A brown tee-shirt is visible at his throat; this has now replaced the older green version for field wear. (Arnold Meisner/*Defense Image*)

83. A soldier of the 101st Airborne Division (Air Assault), clad in a rain jacket over BDUs, during Operation 'Solid Shield', Camp Geiger, North Carolina, May 1983. His protective mask, worn at the 'side-carry' position, and the .45 pistol seem to indicate that he is a vehicle driver (although he may possibly be a troop leader). At the rear, an 82nd Airborne Division Major looks on; the 'flash' on his beret is that worn by the 82nd's staff and support units. (Arnold Meisner/*Defense Image*)

84. Soldiers of the 24th Infantry Division prepare to fire a Stinger anti-aircraft missile during Operation 'Quick Thrust', December 1984. They wear the two-piece rainsuit over the BDU uniform. (Arnold Meisner/*Defense Image*)

85. A soldier of the 8th Infantry Division (Mech.) during 'Reforger 85', wearing the two-piece chemical protective suit, with DH-132 CVC helmet, black rubber overshoes, cold-weather mittens and basic ALICE equipment. Goggles and a white face-mask protect him further from the elements. (Arnold Meisner/*Defense Image*)

86. Soldiers of the 9th Infantry Division (Motorized) deploy with Dragon anti-tank missile, M60 GPMG and M16 and M16/M203 weapons during the 'Border Star 85' manoeuvres at Fort Bliss. They wear M1952 flak vests over two-piece chemical protective suits, and local foliage has been added to their M1 helmets. (Arnold Meisner/*Defense Image*)

85▲   86▼

87. A Military Policeman of the 43rd MP Brigade, shown during 'Reforger 85'. He wears a BDU field jacket with MP brassard and a full-colour helmet liner. The blue-over-red stripe identifies him as assigned to Corps troops, and the '119' identifies his company. A grey US Navy flashlight is attached to his web gear. (Arnold Meisner/*Defense Image*)

88. Starting in 1975, in a move towards greater standardization among the services, the Army and the Navy adopted the Air Force CWU-27 flight suit for their aviation personnel. Here it is worn, with BDU cap, by an Army sergeant at Fort Stewart, Georgia, May 1985. With the adoption of the Air Force coveralls, the Army also adopted the Air Force aircrew name-tag, which is attached to the flight suit with Velcro. The wearer's name, rank and service are displayed below a representation of his Aviator's Badge; to this, the wearer here has attached his unit crest and Armed Forces ID card, the latter probably for security reasons. (Arnold Meisner/*Defense Image*)

89. During combat operations, the Army aviator wears a special armour vest of aluminium oxide ceramic material over his CWU-27 flight suit, and over this an SRU-21 survival vest made of nylon mesh. The SPH-4C helmet is the standard model for Army helicopter pilots. It is a single-visor model, although different visors can be interchanged as the mission dictates. (Steve Zaloga)

90. A close-up of the SRU-21 survival vest. Its pockets contain an emergency radio, a SEEK (Survival, Escape and Evasion Kit), a compass, flares, a signalling mirror and a field dressing. (Arnold Meisner)

91. The SRU-21 vest and SPH-4C helmet from the rear; the backplate of the aircrew body armour is also seen. Pilots' models lack the backplate, as these crewmen sit in armoured seats. The vests provide a very high degree of individual protection, and have occasionally withstood even 12.5mm impacts. The body armour is not worn during peacetime exercises. (Arnold Meisner/*Defense Image*)

88▲   89▼

90▲   91▼

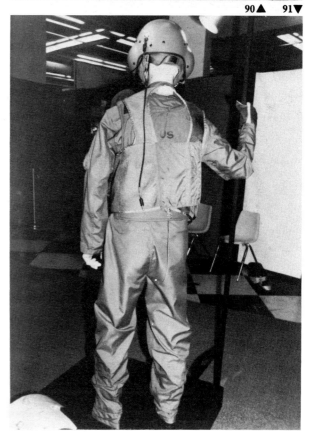

◄92

93▲

◄94

92. A CH-47D Chinook crew chief in the special safety vest worn during special operations such as aerial resupply missions. (Arnold Meisner/*Defense Image*)

93. For cold winter operations, the Army issues the cold-weather parka and field trousers, with liners. This Dragon anti-tank gunner, assigned to 1/58th Infantry during Operation 'Central Guardian' in January 1985, also wears the insulated helmet liner cap. Made in BDU camouflage material, it resembles a bulky toque in shape, and closes with Velcro in front; an older, OD version is also in service. To adjust the sights of his weapon, this gunner has discarded his leather gloves and wears only the wool inserts. (US Army)

94. The cold-weather parka with its fur-trimmed hood up, worn with the older OD helmet liner cap. Notice also the black glove shells worn over the wool inserts. (US Army)

51

▲95　▼96

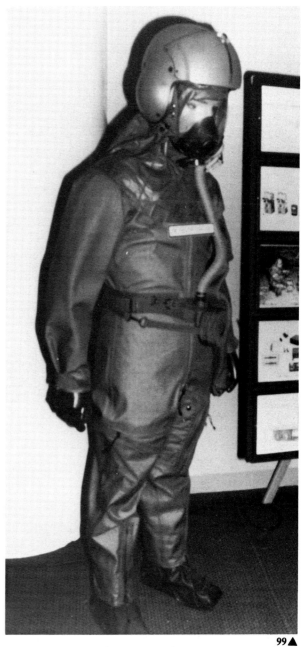

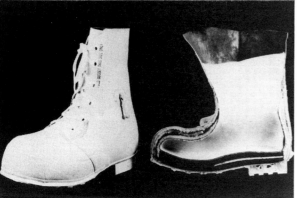

97▲ 98▼

99▲

95. M113 APC crewmen during the 1985 'Reforger' manoeuvres, wearing the winter parka with the DH-132 CVC helmet. (Arnold Meisner/*Defense Image*)

96. M1 Abrams tank crews, with the winter parka and OD helmet liner cap, 'Reforger', 1985. (Arnold Meisner/*Defense Image*)

97. For Arctic conditions, the Army issues a white camouflage parka and trousers for wear over the winter parka. Arctic mittens are retained by the strap as shown, and a white face mask is worn. (Steve Zaloga)

98. The white rubber insulated boot, issued in extreme cold weather for wear with the Arctic camouflage overgarments. A version in black, intended for more moderate climates, also exists. (US Army)

99. NBC protection for aircrews is provided by the ABC-M24 aircraft protective mask, with hood, worn beneath the helmet. It can be connected either to the aircraft's oxygen system or to an oxygen bail-out bottle. Protective gloves and disposable plastic overboots are also worn. While the Army's women pilots are not assigned to combat duties, it is expected that they may have to operate in such an environment. (Steve Zaloga)

◀100　　　　　　　　　　　　　　　　　　　**101▲**

100. For desert operations, the Army's Natick Research and Development Command designed a series of special garments. Here, a paratrooper of the 82nd Airborne Division, during Operation 'Bright Star 82' (a combined exercise with the Egyptian Army), wears the Daytime Desert Uniform. Its cut exactly follows that of the standard BDU, and the 50/50 nylon-cotton fabric incorporates the same anti-infra-red dyes. No special desert camouflage cover was issued, and most units improvised something from tan material (although a daytime desert camouflage cover exists for the 'Fritz' helmet). (US Army via *Defense Image*)
101. The Night Desert Pattern Uniform consists of a parka-style

102▲

overjacket and trousers, which are worn over the Daytime Desert BDU. A hood fits over the 'Fritz' helmet. This uniform is also made of anti-infra-red material: the regular check pattern and uneven 'spots' interfere with the resolution of night-vision devices, which refuse to focus on the material. The uniform is 20 per cent less visible at ranges of less than 100 metres, and completely invisible at ranges of 200 metres or more. (Steve Zaloga)
102. The Army two-piece rainsuit (wet-weather parka and trousers) is issued where the usual rain poncho is either insufficient or will interfere with the soldier's duties. Rubber overshoes are also part of this uniform. (Steve Zaloga)

103. M1 Abrams tank crewmen in Germany, wearing the rainsuit with DH-132 CVC helmets. The soldier on the right wears overall-like US Navy trousers and rainboots, the two soldiers in the centre wear the complete outfit, and the man at the left is wearing the rain jacket with chemical protective trousers. The plastic bag is a protective cover for maps. (Arnold Meisner/*Defense Image*)

104. An M48 Chaparral air defence missile crewman in Germany during field training, wearing the wet-weather jacket with chemical protective trousers. (Arnold Meisner/*Defense Image*)

105. The complete Chemical Protective Ensemble Uniform, consisting of a helmet cover, protective mask, coat, trousers, gloves and footwear covers. A version of this uniform in BDU 'woodland' camouflage material will eventually supplant the OD items in service. Both uniforms are identical in cut, and have outer layers of nylon-cotton fabric and an inner layer of charcoal-impregnated polyurethane foam. The footwear is a sort of laced rubberized bag which fits over the standard combat boot. (US Army)

◀**103**

104▲   105▼

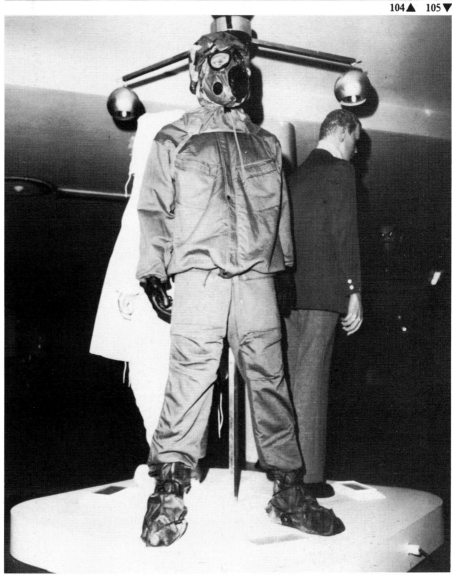

106. The M17A1 protective mask, together with its accompanying hood, is shown in this close-up photograph of a 25th Infantry Division soldier undergoing training in Hawaii. (US Army)

107. The Army will eventually replace the M17 protective mask with the M40 type shown here, worn with the early PASGT helmet and body armour. The M40 offers a number of advantages over the M17, primarily lighter weight and a 'soft' faceplate which allows personnel to get closer to the sights and optical equipment of their weapons. (Steve Zaloga)

108. M577A2 command post vehicle crewmen in Germany, wearing the chemical protective coat and trousers, together with rainboots. Troops usually refer to this suit as 'MOPP gear', after Mission-Oriented Protective Posture, a numerical readiness rating of the unit's preparedness to defend itself against different types of attack. (Arnold Meisner/*Defense Image*)

◄106   107▲   108▼

▲ 109

▼ 110

109. VII Corps self-propelled artillerymen in Germany. They are wearing essentially the Chemical Protective Ensemble Uniform with DH-132 CVC helmets, although the soldier on the right wears the rainsuit instead. (Arnold Meisner/*Defense Image*)

110. The Army's Natick R&D Command has developed a range of other specialized garments for various purposes, such as this protective suit for EOD (Explosive Ordnance Disposal) technicians. (George Balin)

111. Some of the strangest uniforms used by the Army are those worn by members of OPFOR (Opposing Forces) personnel at the National Training Center at Fort Irwin, California, and elsewhere. OPFOR are supposed to simulate Soviet units in training exercises with American troops. Personnel are issued with OG-507 fatigue clothing dyed grey and modified with epaulettes to enable Soviet-style rank insignia to be attached. Black berets are worn by armour crewmen, these soldiers being shown with a simulated SO-152 self-propelled howitzer based on an M551 Sheridan vehicle. Although the Soviets use only full-colour insignia on their uniforms, OPFOR have for some reason produced both full-colour and subdued versions. One soldier, on the right, also wears a dyed M65 field jacket. (US Army)

112. Although OPFOR mainly use converted American vehicles, some Soviet vehicles are available for demonstrations: here, OPFOR infantry disembark from a Soviet BTR-60 APC. Soviet-style shoulder boards and collar tabs decorate the dyed fatigues, a plastic reproduction of the Soviet helmet fits over the M1 helmet liner, and Soviet weapons are carried (black rubber reproductions of these are also available). A tidy individual has also ordered the troops to wear individual name-tags (from the Service Uniform) with their combat dress! (US Army)

113. The Hospital Work Uniform for female Army medical and dental personnel consists of either a white polyester dress or a pantsuit. The white Army Nurse Corps cap is worn indoors, but the standard garrison cap may be worn outside, as shown. Rank and branch devices are worn on the collar, with the name-tag on the right-hand side. (Arnold Meisner/*Defense Image*)

114. Male personnel assigned to duty in Army health care facilities wear the Hospital Duty Uniform, consisting of white smock and trousers. Enlisted personnel wear rank devices on both collars, again with the name-tag on the right-hand side. (Arnold Meisner/*Defense Image*)

115. Military Police wear ordinary Army uniforms, yet, because of their need to maintain a distinctive appearance, they use some unique items of equipment. Here, a male and female MP assigned to Fort McPherson, Georgia, simulate the arrest of a shoplifter. All MPs wear the appropriate Class 'A' or 'B' Uniform in garrison environments, with bloused black combat boots. Male personnel wear the characteristic white hat, while female personnel wear pantsuit uniforms, also with bloused combat boots, and the ordinary service hat. Leather belts, holsters and equipment carriers are also worn. Male MPs carry the .45 pistol, female personnel a .38 revolver, as shown. MPs are allowed to purchase and wear their own equipment, hence the left-handed holster worn by the woman sergeant. (US Army)

116. A black cardigan-style sweater is often worn by indoor workers, medical personnel among them, both male and female. (Arnold Meisner/*Defense Image*)

117. Another view of Fort McPherson MPs. Just visible on the woman sergeant's uniform is the silver MP Badge, worn on all duty uniforms since the early 1960s. The sergeant also wears the women's AG-344 pantsuit, a limited-standard item since the introduction of the Women's 'Classic' Uniform. (US Army)

◄113

114▲ 115▼   116▲ 117▼

118. A woman MP private, wearing Class 'B' Uniform of AG-415 blouse, service hat and the slacks of the AG-344 pantsuit, with bloused combat boots. The MP Badge is, of course, also worn by male MPs. (US Army)

119. An MP officer assigned to the Joint Security Compound Guard at Panmunjom, Korea, wearing an unusual mixture of Class 'B' Uniform with an Air Force N-2B hooded jacket, in sage green with a white acrylic 'fur'-trimmed hood. His metal Parachute Badge and rank device are pinned to a winter 'trooper' hat, a field clothing item that can also be worn with Service Dress. Pinned to the sleeve of his jacket is a black and white MP brassard, an item now worn by MPs only in the field. The subdued shoulder patch of his unit is also worn at the top of the brassard. (Arnold Meisner/*Defense Image*)

120. Military Police from three countries confer during NATO exercises in Germany. The American, second from the right, wears the BDU, basic ALICE items and an M17 protective mask. His black plastic MP brassard displays the white letters 'MP' and the subdued patch of his unit, the 1st Support Brigade. Surprisingly, the slovenly appearance of the bearded *Bundeswehr* soldier on the left attracts little comment in this group. (MoD via *Defense Image*)

◀118   119▲   120▼

121. A cadet officer (his chevrons denoting the rank of Cadet Activities Officer) poses for family photographs during graduation rehearsal, May 1985; he wears Full Dress Grey Over White Uniform Under Arms. In addition to his chevrons, his status as a cadet officer is further indicated by the cock's feather plume (tilted precisely 15 degrees forward), the single crossbelt and the maroon sash gathered on the left side behind his sword – all traditional nineteenth century officers' distinctions. (Arnold Meisner/*Defense Image*)

122. West Point cadets pass in review during Graduation Week ceremonies, June 1978. When the higher-ranking cadet officers graduate, their places are taken in the formation by cadet corporals (double chevron on lower cuffs). Again, the Full Dress Grey Over White Uniform is worn. The three cadet corporals leading the formation, here acting as officers, wear their white waist-belts for the occasion, while several others marching in the ranks behind them are normally accoutred. (US Army)

123. Women were first admitted to the American service academies in July 1976. Many have achieved Cadet Officer rank, and here one of these, a Battalion Adjutant, receives the congratulations of classmates after being awarded her diploma. As can be seen, cadet uniforms make few concessions to women: with the exception of one Evening Mess Uniform, where the women have a floor-length dress, most are identical to the men's. (US Army)

◀121

122▲   123▼

124. With the admission of women in 1976, the service academies had to make a basic decision with regard to uniform policy: whether to design a separate range of women's dress or to try to preserve a homogeneous appearance across the whole Corps of Cadets. As related, they elected to follow the latter approach, in spite of the vaguely 'Ann Miller-ish' appearance that several of the uniforms conveyed. Here, male and female cadets model the Full Dress Grey Winter Uniform. (US Army)

125. Male and female cadets in the double-breasted long overcoat, which was first adopted at West Point in 1851; unlined capes are folded back, according to regulations. In this 1976 photograph the woman cadet wears an experimental black beret, which was eventually dropped in favour of the ordinary grey hat, as worn by her male companion. Several of the women's uniforms have skirt options, and the woman cadet apparently wears that for her Dress Grey Uniform, with black boots. The 'skirt version' of the Dress Grey Uniform is rarely seen, since slacks are usually specified for formations. (US Army)

◄124   125►

126. The Dress Grey Uniform, one of the more famous of the West Point uniforms. Incidentally, the uniform colours of black, grey and gold are intended to be symbolic of the components of gunpowder: charcoal, potassium nitrate and sulphur. (US Army)
127. The Male White Over Grey Uniform. These upper classmen

have qualified as paratroopers during their summer training and are authorized to wear their Parachute Badges with this uniform. The corresponding Women's White Over Grey Uniform consists of a white blouse worn with either grey slacks or a grey skirt. (Arnold Meisner/*Defense Image*)

128. The White Over Grey Uniform Under Arms, worn with white waist- and crossbelts during a 1977 brigade parade. (US Army)

129. West Point cadets under instruction; they wear the Classroom Uniform of dress grey slacks and charcoal grey shirt. After the first year, cadets are allowed to wear the Military Academy crest on their left collars, and, if cadet officers, their metal pin-on rank insignia on their right collars; upper classmen who have not attained officer rank wear pin-on 'US' insignia instead. Their instructor, an Army Artillery captain, wears his Army Green Uniform with the 'USMA' shoulder patch. These few photographs in no way exhaust the subject of West Point uniforms. (US Army)

▲128 ▼129